I0521161

50 Days for Our Father
A Mystagogy on the Lord's Prayer

Br. Gregory Armstrong, O.F.M. Cap.

CAPUCHIN
FRANCISCANS

Denver, CO

Cover Art: *Renunciation of Worldly Goods* by Giotto. The Frescos of
the Saint Francis cycle in the Upper Church of San Francesco in
Assisi attributed to Giotto di Bondone and replicated in the present
work are Public Domain images, used via Wikimedia Commons.

Published by the Capuchin Province of Mid-America
3613 Wyandot St., Denver, CO 80211

ISBN-13: 979-8-9941258-0-9

CONTENTS

ILLUSTRATIONS

Acknowledgements

Thanks be to God the Father, for the gift of salvation in his Son Jesus Christ! I also thank the parishioners and staff at St. Padre Pio Parish in San Antonio, TX, who encouraged me to go deeper into the *Our Father* by developing catechetical sessions on the Lord's Prayer. Likewise, this project would not have been undertaken without the support and assistance of the brothers of my Capuchin Province of Mid-America.

i

Author's Note

This little book is a text adaptation of a series of prayers I presented as a daily video series during Easter 2025. These short prayers respond to a real need in the Church today: the recovery of Easter Mystagogy. Indeed, it was in the context of studying the revised Order of Christian Initiation and the Catholic Church's ancient tradition of providing ongoing spiritual formation to neophytes that I conceived of this 50-day format (so numbered as to match the number of days in Eastertide). That said, I pray that the daily prayers and their culmination in oblation to the Father may be found of value to any Christian, not just newly initiated Catholics.

Introduction

In the heart of Assisi, a young man takes a step that will prove pivotal. Before his father, before the bishop, before the whole town, Francis of Assisi strips himself of everything: his clothes, his inheritance, his very name. In this moment, naked in body but free in soul, he turns his gaze to heaven and prays: 'No longer do I say my father, Pietro Bernardone, but Our Father, who art in Heaven...'

This action was not the beginning of St. Francis' conversion, nor was it its completion. He had already embraced the leper. He had already heard Christ's call from San Damiano: *Rebuild my Church*. On the other hand, he had yet to meet his brothers, yet to preach before a Sultan, yet to suffer and rejoice in ways he could not imagine. He lived in the tension between what had already begun and what was yet to come.

Is this not where we find ourselves: the already-but-not-yet of conversion? In response, we pray. *50 Days with Our Father* is an invitation to pray through the Lord's Prayer and to experience this formulation not as words to be stated, but rather as yearnings to be prayed. Each day, a short text, rooted in one of the petitions of the *Our Father*, will guide us in prayer, drawing us deeper into trust, surrender, and belonging as sons and daughters of God.

For fifty days, from Easter Sunday to Pentecost, the Church walks with the risen Christ. Each day, we will pause to pray, offering our hearts to the Father, through the Son in the Spirit. We will take up the words Christ himself gave us and learn to make them our own.

From the earliest days of the Church, these fifty days were set aside for mystagogy; they were a sacred opportunity to be led deeper into the mysteries already received. The newly baptized, together with those who had long walked the way of faith, would reflect on the sacraments they had received, on the prayers they had learned, and on the life of grace that had been opened to them. The *Our Father* was at the heart of this formation because to pray it is to enter into the life of the Son.

Wherever you are in your journey, whether prayer is your daily bread or something you struggle to begin, you are invited. Pray with us. Walk with us: each day, set aside a short moment of reflection. Then, when we arrive at Pentecost, we will make an act of oblation—an offering of ourselves to the Father, in the Son, through the Spirit. This consecration is a simple yet profound act of entrustment; the hope is that at the end of these fifty days, you will not just know the *Our Father* but will have learned to surrender yourself through it into the hands of our loving Father.

To get the most out of this book, I enjoin the reader, whether neophyte or life-long Christian, to set aside some time each day to slowly pray the day's text and meditate on the part of the Lord's Prayer which inspired it. So doing, you may begin (or advance in) the practice of mental prayer.

Lastly, I recommend accompanying these days with another resource which comments on the *Our Father* in a more discursive way. Among the many books, catechetical series, and productions expounding the *Our Father*, I suggest that Part IV of the Catechism of the Catholic Church enjoys a singular esteem.

As we draw our inspiration from St. Francis' action, let us begin by praying his own *Prayer Inspired by the Our Father:*

O ***Our Father*** most holy:
Our Creator, Redeemer, Consoler, and Savior:

Who are in heaven:
In the angels and the saints,
enlightening them to know, for *You, Lord, are light;*
inflaming them to love, for You, Lord, are love;
dwelling in them and filling them with happiness,
for You, Lord, are Supreme Good, the Eternal Good,
from Whom all good comes
without Whom there is no good.

Holy be Your Name:
May knowledge of You become clearer in us
that we may know
the breadth of Your blessings,
the length of Your promises
the height of Your majesty,
the depth of Your judgments.

Your kingdom come:
That You may rule in us through Your grace
and enable us *to come* to *Your kingdom*
where there is clear vision of You,
perfect love of You,
blessed companionship with You,
eternal enjoyment of You.

Your will be done on earth as in heaven:
That we may love You
with our whole heart by always thinking of You,
with our whole strength by exerting
all our energies and affections of body and soul
in the service of Your love and of nothing else;
and we may love our neighbor as ourselves
by drawing them all to Your love with our whole
strength,
by rejoicing in the good of others as in our own,
by suffering with others at their misfortunes,
and by giving offense to no one.

Give us this day:
in remembrance, understanding, and reverence
of that love which our Lord Jesus Christ had for us
and of those things that He said
and did and suffered for us.

our daily bread:
Your own beloved Son, our Lord Jesus Christ.

Forgive us our trespasses:
through Your ineffable mercy
through the power of the passion of Your beloved Son
and through the merits and intercession
of the ever-blessed Virgin and all Your elect.

As we forgive those who trespass against us:
And what we do not completely forgive,
make us, Lord, forgive completely
that we may truly love our enemies because of You
and we may fervently intercede for them before You,
returning no one evil for evil
and we may strive to help everyone in You.

And lead us not into temptation:
hidden or obvious,
sudden or persistent.

But deliver us from evil:
past,
present,
and to come.

Glory to the Father,
and to the Son,
and to the Holy Spirit.
As it was in the beginning,
is now,
and will be forever.
Amen.[1]

---

[1] You may desire to return to this prayer at other points through-out these fifty days, and I would encourage you to do so. This translation of St. Francis' prayer is found in *Francis of Assisi: Early Documents*, vol. I, ed. Regis J. Armstrong, J. A. Wayne Hellmann, and William J. Short (New City Press: New York, 1999), 158-160.

6

Our Father,
Who art in Heaven

Day 1: Lord, Teach us how to Pray

How many times did the disciples see Jesus wander off or disappear up a mountain to be alone with His Father in prayer? These disciples, who followed Jesus so closely and so lovingly, must have wondered at the intimacy the Son of Man shared with His Heavenly Father. In their wonder, they began to desire to partake in that relationship of love with the Father. And so, they entreated Christ:

"Lord, teach us to pray."

Lord Jesus, your response is the summary of the Gospel. You teach us Your own prayer—the Lord's Prayer, the *Our Father*.

In this prayer is contained everything for which we Christians ought to pray, everything we Christians ought to desire, and the order in which they are to be desired. Thus, you, Lord, taught your first disciples—and teach us now—to begin by turning our gaze in worship to the Father. After resting in the glory of His magnificence, we are assured that all our needs are cared for by His providence, that we might go forth in charity.

We are invited to first lay aside our cares by entering into relationship with the Father.

Then, we allow Him to take up our cares: to meet our daily needs, forgive us our sins, and lead us finally home to Him.

We turn first to God the Father, then go forth in love. These words are a model of prayer and a model of life. Who but you, Lord, could reveal such a way?

Only the Way, the Truth, the Life.

Only the Revelation of the Father in the Firstborn Son turned our Brother.

Only the God-Man, the fullness of Revelation.

The great mystery of Revelation! The God who made us came to meet us. The Word, in whom we were spoken into being, returns us to the Father who spoke and speaks His being from all eternity.

So now, we may begin to say:

Our Father, who art in Heaven
Hallowed be thy name.
Thy kingdom come,
thy will be done,
on earth as it is in heaven.
Give us this day our daily bread,
And forgive us our trespasses,
as we forgive those who trespass against us.
Lead us not into temptation,
But deliver us from evil.
Amen.

Day 2: The Summary of the Gospel

The *Our Father* is the summary of the Gospel. This prayer has, from ancient times, been used to further and complete the formation of those who enter the Church at the Easter Vigil. It is a source and font of mystical guidance, an initiation to Gospel living.

Father, so that we might fully understand the significance of this claim, clarify for us one thing: What is the Gospel? What is the good news of Jesus Christ?

In Jesus—the Son of God and the Son of Man—relationship with You, Father, is once again on the table. St. Paul tells us that in Adam, all sinned. But what is this sin of Adam, this original sin? It is the inability to be in relationship with You, God, our Creator and Father.

We should not think of original sin—which is wiped away in baptism—on a purely individual basis. It is not a personal defect, something that can be detected in any one person in isolation. No, it is rather the loss of relationship, a severing of the bond between God and humanity. Original sin is not a fact of imperfection but a state of isolation.

But in Jesus Christ, the God-Man, this relationship has been restored. What the first Adam lost, the new Adam won. What the first Adam squandered when he plucked the fruit of the tree of the knowledge of good and evil, the new Adam, Jesus Christ, regained for all upon the tree of life, the Cross.

This is the good news: In the Son, we are now adopted as sons and daughters of You, Father. We prodigals have been won back by the love of our Beloved. By His suffering and death, His hanging upon the tree, we have been brought and bought back to life in You!

And what is this life? It is the life-giving relationship with You, Father. In our baptism, we have already been grafted onto this tree of life. What remains for us now is to live the Gospel life.

So, what is the Gospel, the good news? We have been restored to relationship with You, our Creator God.

And what is that relationship? In Jesus Christ, the Firstborn Son, we are adopted sons and daughters of the Father to whom we now pray in filial boldness:

Our Father, who art in Heaven
Hallowed be thy name.
Thy kingdom come,
thy will be done,
on earth as it is in heaven.
Give us this day our daily bread,
And forgive us our trespasses,
as we forgive those who trespass against us.
Lead us not into temptation,
But deliver us from evil.
Amen.

Day 3: "Our"

Lord, Jesus, the message of your prayer is clear from the beginning: God is our Father.

Yes, He is our Father as I write this, and He is our Father as you read it. Do we say, "*My* Father, who art in heaven?" No, we say *Our* Father. You, Lord, our Christ, taught us to say this.

Why "our" and not "my"?

The ability to call God "Father," the fact that we can dare to make such a claim, is the result of the relationship restored by You, the Son. We have become members of Your Body—the Body of the Christ. And while this membership is deeply personal, it is not isolated nor solely individual. You, Christ, are the firstborn of many brothers and sisters, the Head of the Body, the Church.

If we can pray boldly to the Father, if we can dare to declare this patrimony, we cannot dare it alone. The very fact of our new family requires us to recognize it in the word *our*, rather than *my*.

This death-won relationship with the Father and the Son through the Spirit is not solely a personal possession. It is not my property. Rather, it is a sharing in the communion of the Lord. You thus teach us that, when we pray, we begin with this recognition of communion in mind.

Thus, I cannot say "My Father," because I would not be able to call God "Father" if it were not for You, my brother, Jesus Christ. When I pray to the Father, I must always pray "our" along with You, the Christ, the Son, my firstborn brother.

But it doesn't stop there. I cannot pray to the Father with You alone. How could I pray with my eldest brother while excluding the rest of His Body, the Church?

Anytime we pray as Christians, we pray in and with You, our brother Jesus and in and with Your Body, the Church.

And so, let us not say "My Father," but:

> *Our Father, who art in Heaven*
> *Hallowed be thy name.*
> *Thy kingdom come,*
> *thy will be done,*
> *on earth as it is in heaven.*
> *Give us this day our daily bread,*
> *And forgive us our trespasses,*
> *as we forgive those who trespass against us.*
> *Lead us not into temptation,*
> *But deliver us from evil.*
> *Amen.*

Day 4: "Father"

We have spoken of the word "our," and now we turn to "Father." What does it mean to call You, God, our Father? Fatherhood, as revealed to us, finds its primary reference in You. You are the ultimate and perfect Father: unlimited, providential, and unchanging. You are a rock on which we can build, the source of our very life. You nurture us, guide us, protect us, and give us the freedom to flourish in response to the gifts You have so generously given.

Yet, our earthly fathers often fall short of Your perfect image. Limited by their humanity and materiality, they provide only an imperfect reflection of fatherhood. They abscond, abuse, or damage where You nurture. It is easier for us to view fatherhood through the flawed examples we see, but even the most faithful and loving earthly fathers are more dissimilar to You than they are similar.

Sadly, then, our image of fatherhood is deformed by their example. But we can and must purify and heal it through relationship with You. You are Father from eternity. My own father is a father only in time. You are the Father of all creation; my own father is the father of me alone. And yet, in Your transcendence and all-encompassing glory, You know the number of the hairs on my head. You do not forget the smallest sparrow or the lilies in the field. You are truly Father.

Help us, good Father, to know true fatherhood in Your person. Only by knowing You can we begin to understand our own nature as Your children. Do we truly believe that we are sons and daughters in the one Son, Jesus Christ—the eternally begotten Word of the Father, the perfect image of the Father Himself? To a certain extent, I am an image of my earthly father. We all bear the image of those who begot us. Yet Jesus Christ is the perfect image of You, Father. Is this what it means to be begotten? To be born anew in water and Spirit? To become an image of the Father's love on earth?

Yes, this is what it means to be Your child: to live as an image of You, as Jesus Christ does perfectly. To live as Your child is to walk in the footprints of Christ, to reflect His excellence. By His grace, we are formed into faithful likenesses of You. You, the divine Artist, through your love, make us your children, so that we may dare to say:

*Our **Father**, who art in Heaven*
Hallowed be thy name.
Thy kingdom come,
thy will be done,
on earth as it is in heaven.
Give us this day our daily bread,
And forgive us our trespasses,
as we forgive those who trespass against us.
Lead us not into temptation,
But deliver us from evil.
Amen.

15

Day 5: In Heaven Only?

Where Are You, Father?

Father, where are You?

The Son has come to Bethlehem, with the mission to make You known.

The Son has gone to Calvary, to make us Your own.

The Son rose on the third day after death, to give us hope.

The Son walked, ate, and displayed His wounds, but then He had to go.

The Son returned to Your side, to rule in heavenly might.

Father, now I ask: Where is heaven's light?

Our firstborn Brother, Your beloved Son, taught us to pray: "Our Father, who art in heaven." But Father, what does it mean for You to be in heaven? It cannot mean You are far away, distant from my cause.

It cannot mean You have run away, leaving me with flaws.

"Our Father, who art in heaven." Our Father, who art the very place of our blessedness. This is what we proclaim. Our Father, You are our ultimate goal, the end toward which our gaze is turned. When our Lord taught us to pray, He told us to begin by fixing our eyes on our end—Your side, where He ascends.

Our Father, You are not far. You dwell within our hearts. And yet, You are also truly in heaven. You are the goal, the end, the resting place, toward which our love must always tend.

And so, as we begin to pray, as we glorify Your name, we recall and yearn for the destination of our earthly pilgrimage. We are not meant to stay down here below. We are meant to be raised up at Your side. Not left abandoned or alone, but brought to You:

*Our Father, **who art in Heaven***
Hallowed be thy name.
Thy kingdom come,
thy will be done,
on earth as it is in heaven.
Give us this day our daily bread,
And forgive us our trespasses,
as we forgive those who trespass against us.
Lead us not into temptation,
But deliver us from evil.
Amen.

Hallowed be Thy Name

Day 6: Thy Name

What's in a Name?

A name communicates mission. We've all known Bakers, Carpenters, or Smiths—a name connotes vocation.

A name communicates identity: it picks out this one, and not another.

A name communicates being.

A name is not just a word; it is something of the person. When someone shares their name with us, they reveal something of themselves. In human relationships, this revelation can be small or profound. And we are not always exactly what our name claims.

God, however, is what He is. He is *who* He is. God's name communicates His very self. To know the name of God is to know Him.

Father, You have revealed Your name to us gradually through history. Why was this revelation necessary? Once, we walked with You in the garden, but our first parents fell from their natural state of grace and relationship with You. Humanity forgot the name of the One to whom they owed their very being.

Yet, miracle of miracles, what we had claimed for

ourselves—our lives—You did not leave to us alone. You came back into our story.

You revealed Yourself to the patriarchs and prophets. To Moses, You said, "I am who am." You became the God of Abraham, Isaac, and Jacob—the God of Israel.

What is Your name? Wonder-Counselor, God-Warrior, Father-Forever, Prince of Peace?

The fullness of the revelation of Your name came in the fullness of Your very Godhead: Jesus Christ, the Word made flesh, the Son of the Father. God is with us! He came to save us from our sins. And even if we had not sinned, He still would have come—to reveal the full mystery of Your name:

> *Our Father, who art in Heaven*
> *Hallowed be **thy name**.*
> *Thy kingdom come,*
> *thy will be done,*
> *on earth as it is in heaven.*
> *Give us this day our daily bread,*
> *And forgive us our trespasses,*
> *as we forgive those who trespass against us.*
> *Lead us not into temptation,*
> *But deliver us from evil.*
> *Amen.*

Day 7: To Hallow

Oh Jesus, our brother, You revealed the name of the Father. You revealed the name of God as Trinity—Yourself, the second Person. We pray that Your Divine and triune name might be hallowed across all the earth. Hallowed, hallowed, hallowed be Thy name—through Jesus, the Lord, the Image of the Father.

Father, how can Your name be hallowed? Is it not already holy? Your name is good, true, beautiful, and perfect. Your name is justice and mercy. Your name is peace. Is Your name not already as holy as can be? Why, then, do we say, "Hallowed be Thy name"? The answer cannot be found in You, for You are unchanging. It must be a change within us—a conversion of our hearts.

Yes, Father, when we pray, "Hallowed be Thy name," We ask that Your name might be recognized as holy in our hearts, on our tongues, in our minds, by our desires, and in our lives.

We do not cause Your name to be holy.

We pray instead that we might truly recognize it as such. And not only us, Father. The good Lord Jesus did not teach us to say, "Hallowed be Thy name by those who already call upon it." No, He said simply, "Hallowed be Thy name." There is no limit, no qualification. Not for a certain people, or a certain time in history. We pray that in every place, in every age, in every heart, on every tongue, Your name, Father, might be known as holy. For if Your name is seen as hallowed, then You, too, will be known and loved. So, Father, we pray for ourselves and for all peoples: Hallowed be Your name. Hallowed be Your name, You who are:

Our Father, who art in Heaven
Hallowed *be thy name.*
Thy kingdom come,
thy will be done,
on earth as it is in heaven.
Give us this day our daily bread,
And forgive us our trespasses,
as we forgive those who trespass against us.
Lead us not into temptation,
But deliver us from evil.
Amen.

Thy Kingdom Come

Day 8: The Ancient Kingdom

What mysterious kingdom lies behind our second plea? We are told to pray by our King that His kingdom may come. What kingdom do we pray for? What King do we await? Why do we pray your kingdom to come?

In olden times, you revealed your name, O God, identifying yourself as the God of Abraham, Isaac, and Israel. From Israel were born 12 tribes, descendants of Abraham, multiplied beyond number—more numerous than the sands of the seashore. These 12 sons and their families were your first historical kingdom, with you as their King.

In times of need, you gave them judges, instruments of your salvation. But there came a day when they remembered not that you were the Father of their people. They glanced about and saw, on every side, worldly peoples with human kings. They said to Samuel, their last good judge: "Pray to the Lord our God to give us a king."

Samuel tore his garments and bemoaned their misguided plea. But you, Lord, looked upon him and said: "Be not distressed; they reject not you, but me." You promised them a king and warned them of what this would bring—a king like any other nation, who would take their sons to die in wars and their daughters to serve his desires. Knowing this, the people of Israel still clamored for a human, fallen king.

You gave them Saul, who quickly failed. Yet you, O God, would not abandon your people, even in their folly. You gave them David, and to David, you promised an eternal kingdom. In time, that kingdom, too, seemed to disappear. But through the prophets, you foretold that a new King would come, to restore what had been lost.

Brought low by internal strife and external oppression, your people yearned for salvation. We, too, in our lives, face turmoil and fear. We, like ancient Israel, afraid and seeking help, glance nervously around us in the world, and we notice the earthly kingdoms. We forget *thy* kingdom, and we accept a ruler like any other; we comfort ourselves by crying out "*My* Kingdom!"

But you, our Father, know the King we need. You have given us this King in time, the one who fulfills your promises and reigns eternally. And so, finally, we do not pray "*my* kingdom come," but "*thy* kingdom come."

Our Father, who art in Heaven
Hallowed be thy name.
Thy kingdom come,
thy will be done,
on earth as it is in heaven.
Give us this day our daily bread,
And forgive us our trespasses,
as we forgive those who trespass against us.
Lead us not into temptation,
But deliver us from evil.
Amen.

Day 9: The Firstborn King

In Bethlehem is born a babe—a newborn King. What kingdom does he come to claim? With whose kingship does he reign?

The tribes' poignant longing, the hope of all peoples, is now fulfilled in this person. The Son of David comes in poverty to save us from our sin. David's *basileia* is forged anew in him, revealing a triple reality: new kingship, new kingdom, new reign.

The new kingship, built from the ruins of David, is given over to Christ: the power to govern, to order, and to restore all creation to the Father. The new kingdom he establishes is concrete and historical, yet not political—a new spiritual Israel born from Daughter Zion, the fruitful Virgin Mary.

The Firstborn lies in Bethlehem with a mission to redeem. He comes to give us the gift of adoption as His many brothers and sisters, the subjects of his kingdom.

But let us not be tricked into thinking that this kingship and kingdom are merely "things." No, they are also an Act. The reign of God has come among us— God's action breaking into history. The promised eternal Reign is fulfilled in the saving activity of the Son of Man, the Son of Our Father.

Oh Jesus, Thy *basileia* come! Thy kingship, thy kingdom, thy reign come! Come, You Yourself, Son of:

> *Our Father, who art in Heaven*
> *Hallowed be thy name.*
> **Thy kingdom come,**
> *thy will be done,*
> *on earth as it is in heaven.*
> *Give us this day our daily bread,*
> *And forgive us our trespasses,*
> *as we forgive those who trespass against us.*
> *Lead us not into temptation,*
> *But deliver us from evil.*
> *Amen.*

Day 10: The Ecclesial Kingdom

Father, where lives thy kingdom now? Where acts thy reign?

You established the kingdom in the person of your Son, Jesus Christ. He ascended back to you—for what reason or purpose did he ascend? He tells us it was so that he could send the Spirit among us.

When the Spirit alighted at Pentecost upon those gathered in prayer with Mary, your perfect Daughter, what new creation was brought about? The Spirit came to be the breath of life. Jesus is the life, His is the body, yet also we are the body, now animated by the Spirit. The Spirit breathes so that we may have life.

Into what were those disciples formed? From Paul, we know they were made into the Body—the Church— which even now persists through the ages. Scarred and torn, yet always vanquishing, she is never conquered. Your gift, the Church, with many members who share many gifts and charisms, remains united as your Body.

The kingdom came in your Son's person; the Church is His mystical person persisting today in the world. If He is the Light of the nations, the Church is now the bearer of this Light to all peoples.

The answer becomes clear: Thy kingdom come, thy Church be well.

Father, we pray then, thy kingdom come: We pray for the Church on earth in all ages and all places. May your kingdom come to reign in the hearts of every people. The Church exists to evangelize, to bear your kingdom to all, so we pray for her now with the words you gave us:

Our Father, who art in Heaven
Hallowed be thy name.
Thy kingdom come,
thy will be done,
on earth as it is in heaven.
Give us this day our daily bread,
And forgive us our trespasses,
as we forgive those who trespass against us.
Lead us not into temptation,
But deliver us from evil.
Amen.

Day 11: Incarnation

Three times the kingdom comes, three times the King advents. First, and fully, the Word became Flesh. This Flesh promised to remain with us to the end of the age, even after ascending back to the Father. His presence advents, secondly and continuingly, in the Eucharist, daily bread for the journey. Yet even this journey is not the end, for the Flesh will come again, a third time at the consummation of time.

Father, what a mystery you present to us! The first mission within the very Godhead—the procession of the Son—is mirrored in your creation, for whose consummation the Second Person was sent into the world. Oh, sublime humility! Humble sublimity! That God, the Maker of all things, should become one of us, should walk among us as a man, should know all our pains and sufferings, and be like us in every way but sin!

We cannot claim a distant God who knows not our concerns. We cannot claim an abstract God when this concreteness of Flesh bears living witness before us.

No, for, you, our beloved Jesus, have enfleshed yourself in history, becoming our brother.

In history, you came to be our Savior.

In history, you came to be our Way.

In history, you came to be our Life.

In history, you came to give your life.

This is the awe-inspiring, astounding truth: the God of all consolation tore the temple veil. You did not remain removed from us when we cast you off through sin but instead chose to walk among us. The first coming of the kingdom is You, Jesus Christ, the God-Man. Do we know, then, that when we pray, "Our Father, thy kingdom come," we beg for, we worship, the Son becoming man, whose Incarnation opens the Way for us to pray:

Our Father, who art in Heaven
Hallowed be thy name.
Thy kingdom come,
thy will be done,
on earth as it is in heaven.
Give us this day our daily bread,
And forgive us our trespasses,
as we forgive those who trespass against us.
Lead us not into temptation,
But deliver us from evil.
Amen.

Day 12: Eucharistic Kingdom

Behold I will remain with you even until the end of the Age.

This is what you told us, good Lord, faithful King. Even as you, at the completion of first coming, prepared to return to the Father and send the Spirit, you promised to continue to be present with us here below. And this must be the case...how could the Kingdom reign eternal if it was left unhelmed? How could the people persevere if they became cut off from their King?

But how do You remain, good King? We pray the Father that his Kingdom come, but was it not already established in your incarnation? Why continue the prayer, unless we are praying for a deepening of your presence, a perseverance and permanence of the Kingdom in the world?

What deeper meaning, then, is there in this prayer?

We beg for, we believe in, we beseech you to make your Kingship, your Kingdom, your Reign take hold of us now! But how, if not through your very presence? It must be, then, by your very presence even today that your Kingdom comes. And your true presence is still here among us, we do believe. Not just a metaphor, not a symbol, but your whole and entire person stays present among us till the end of the age. On every altar, in the hands of every priest, in each holy reception by our Catholic souls, your Eucharistic Presence reigns.

Where are you today, Lord? Where is your throne from which you establish your Kingdom daily anew? You rule from underneath the cover of the humble bodily clay of those who profess "Lord I am not worthy that you should enter under my roof, but only say the word and my soul shall be healed."

Only say the word and your Kingdom shall persevere in us.

Only say the word and we will be your brothers and sisters, who together say:

Our Father, who art in Heaven
Hallowed be thy name.
Thy kingdom come,
thy will be done,
on earth as it is in heaven.
Give us this day our daily bread,
And forgive us our trespasses,
as we forgive those who trespass against us.
Lead us not into temptation,
But deliver us from evil.
Amen.

Day 13: Come Again

Father, thy kingdom hath come, initially in the Incarnation: the only begotten Son, our firstborn brother, the Lord and King, Jesus the Christ. Father, thy kingdom comes still today in every Mass, the continuation of the eldest Son's presence in the Eucharist—Body, Blood, Soul, and Divinity—brought down from heaven in the hands of the priest, received on the tongues of even the least.

Yet still we pray, Thy kingdom come.

One more advent must take place.

Our good King will come again to judge the living and the dead. When we glance around, when we look deeply into the world in which we ourselves are found, we see that though the kingdom has broken onto earth, the reign of God is not fully realized in the hearts of every man—not fully realized even in the hearts of us who claim to stand with him.

When we look at the world—though it is not ours to judge—we see both goats and sheep. We clearly see the divided land, torn between the City of God and the city of man. And so we know: the King must come to rain down justice and mercy, to place some to his left and some to his right. It is not ours to judge, ourselves or another. It is ours to hope in His merciful love. We pray: Come again, Lord Jesus. Father, send the Son. Bring final peace into the world. Let us be judged not on the basis of the evils we have done, but on what your merits have won. Let no longer strife and discord, division and hate have any place in your creation.

But come again, Lord Jesus. Quickly, Jesus, come. Draw us finally to the Father's side and delay no longer. Delay no longer. Please, Lord Jesus, come.

And so we pray with ardent hope to the one who sent You first,

Our Father, who art in Heaven
Hallowed be thy name.
*Thy kingdom **come**,*
thy will be done,
on earth as it is in heaven.
Give us this day our daily bread,
And forgive us our trespasses,
as we forgive those who trespass against us.
Lead us not into temptation,
But deliver us from evil.
Amen.

Day 14: Maranatha!

Come, Spirit, Reveal Our Hearts

Come, Spirit, reveal to us our hearts. The kingdom come, thy kingdom come.

We've said it many times. But do we really yearn to let God order our lives? Do I really—do we really—wish to stand before the Father's face? Do we really wish to occupy the heavenly space?

What darkened thoughts, what harsh desires, what apathies and tragedies prevent our hearts from sincerely seeking that for which we pray?

Come, Spirit, now remove all fear.

Come, Spirit, now.

Come, Spirit, now. Enlighten the darkness of our feeble minds. Grant light unto our inner eyes, that we may fix our gaze upon the One whom we so often praise.

Grant us a glimpse of the Author of Love. Grant us again a glimpse of the life in heaven above, that seeing what the Father has planned, our wills may yearn more ardently for that heavenly land.

Come, Spirit, grant us breath anew, with which to speak the words of praise: Our Father, hallowed be thy name. Our Father, may thy kingdom come. Our Father,

thank you for the Son. Our Father, extend His reign—
even, and especially, to the parts of my heart, to the parts
of our hearts, which we still restrain, which still refrain
from being lit by love.

Our Father, who art in Heaven
Hallowed be thy name.
*Thy kingdom **come**,*
thy will be done,
on earth as it is in heaven.
Give us this day our daily bread,
And forgive us our trespasses,
as we forgive those who trespass against us.
Lead us not into temptation,
But deliver us from evil.
Amen.

Thy Will be Done

Day 15: God's Will

Father, we now pray that your will may be done on earth as it is in heaven. Help us to know your will—to know your will with the knowledge that rests in love and leads to love.

Your will is love.

How could knowledge of it lead us to anything other than love? It is true that seeing your will is not enough; seeing, we must also be transformed. But first, let us see. Let us contemplate. Let us be enraptured by the goodness of your will.

Yes, Father, you are good—all good, every good, totally good.

In us, the will is that which tends toward the good. Your will is simply good, for you are simply good. Your love, your tending to the good, is fulfilled totally in yourself. You are both the infinite object of love and the infinite subject that loves. Father, you are good love. You are loving good, totally satisfied in yourself.

In your superabundant goodness, in the fecundity of your love, the Son proceeds and the Spirit spirates. This community of Lover, Beloved, and the Third with whom to share the love—while sufficient in itself—is superabundant in its unity and fecundity. The triune love pours forth. Goodness overflows. You will creation. You love creation. And thus, you will that creation would ultimately return to you.

You predestined us for glory. Yes, Father, foreknowing that which you created in utter goodness and fecundity, you predestine it. You call it. You justify it. You will that it be glorified.

What is your will?

Your will is that which loves us into being at every moment.

Your will is that which sent your Son so that, after our human family had fallen, we might be given justice in the Just One. In your mercy, you will that we might be just. You will that we might have grace to run the glorious race.

Our Father, who art in Heaven
Hallowed be thy name.
Thy kingdom come,
thy will *be done,*
on earth as it is in heaven.
Give us this day our daily bread,
And forgive us our trespasses,
as we forgive those who trespass against us.
Lead us not into temptation,
But deliver us from evil.
Amen.

Day 16: Transcendence

Father, even as you create us moment by moment in your loving Goodness, do you not stand infinitely beyond us? We say again, grant us sight of your will, so that seeing your desire, our own may burn with truer love. But how can we contemplate something so beyond us, a love beyond all telling, the greatest possible goodness? Grant us but a glimpse of your infinite good-will!

Your will is good, your will is true, your will is just and merciful. Good beyond goodness, truer than true, most mercifully just. Our limited language must fail on the approach of your transcendence, so grant us grace to draw near in knowledge and love! You who are greater-than-can-be-conceived, help us to approach you-than-which-nothing-greater-can-be-thought!

We must gently lay aside the bounds of our concepts, to clarify our clouded eyes.

You are Good, for as your Son has said: only God is good. Are you that good which is good only for a while, from a certain point in time? No, for we can think that you would be better if you were good from the beginning. Then will your goodness ever end? This too, must not be the case, your goodness must extend always. Even here, we remain far off, for why must your goodness begin and extend, why should it not simply be from eternity, from that glimpse of all time outside of time? Your goodness must be so good as to not be a possession of time, even if it permeates all time, for you are the author of time.

And so with truth.

And so with merciful justice.

And so with love.

You are you, you rest above and below, within and without our earthly minds' darkened gaze. Oh, be our light, you heavenly Lover, that we might begin to approach your goodness! We know you will to be seen, for you revealed yourself to us, your children, so we confidently pray: grant us the darkness of being blinded in your light,

Our Father, who art in Heaven
Hallowed be thy name.
Thy kingdom come,
thy will be done,
on earth as it is in heaven.
Give us this day our daily bread,
And forgive us our trespasses,
as we forgive those who trespass against us.
Lead us not into temptation,
But deliver us from evil.
Amen.

Day 17: Four Harmonies

Father, we long to know your will, to love your will, and to love in and through your will. Why do we find ourselves so dark, so bent over, blind, and mute before you? Why is it so difficult to stand upright, to fly with the vision of our minds into the depths of your love?

Why can't we love?

When the harmonies were made discordant by sin—creation, self, others, and you—when our first parents chose not to trust, when their love for you died in the face of fear and deceit, the symphony of fourfold harmony became a relational cacophony.

But this was not as you willed it. You willed concord, not discord. You made creation a temple for yourself, and you made us your royal priests—to love the temple, to love each other, to love you.

But instead of seeking and receiving the one fruit of love, we grasped, at the torment of that ancient foe—the devil, for the knowledge of good and evil.

Yet in the fullness of time, you sent your Son—not only to restore our ability, our capacity, and our fulfillment in loving you, but also to restore our ability, our capacity, our desire to love all of the beautiful creation around us, to love our neighbors as ourselves, and finally, the most difficult of all, to love ourselves *in you.*

And so, let us begin to love again as we say:

Our Father, who art in Heaven
Hallowed be thy name.
Thy kingdom come,
thy will be done,
on earth as it is in heaven.
Give us this day our daily bread,
And forgive us our trespasses,
as we forgive those who trespass against us.
Lead us not into temptation,
But deliver us from evil.
Amen.

On Earth as it is in Heaven

Day 18: The Veil Torn

Father, we pray that your will be done on earth as it is in heaven.

But where do earth and heaven meet?

Where is the veil torn?

When your Son died upon Calvary, sighing his last breath, the veil that stands between your love and our hardened hearts was torn. As the temple veil was rent in two, your love was revealed. The earth quaked. Heaven thundered. The barrier was peeled back.

Where today is that veil-tearing reality perpetuated, re-presented?

At the Mass.

In the one sacrifice of Christ, here on our altar—an altar made of earth—we meet the God of heaven, reconciled by the great bridge of Christ's dying and now undying love.

Father, you willed to reconcile us to yourself, so you gave us your only begotten Son—who, once for all, offers himself, and yet whom you make available to us at every Eucharist.

Father, give us your Son as our daily bread, the bread that fulfills your will on earth, just as it is in heaven.

Our Father, who art in Heaven
Hallowed be thy name.
Thy kingdom come,
thy will be done,
on earth as it is in heaven.
Give us this day our daily bread,
And forgive us our trespasses,
as we forgive those who trespass against us.
Lead us not into temptation,
But deliver us from evil.
Amen.

Day 19: Chariots of Flame

Father, you once granted the prophet Elisha the grace to witness you catching Elijah up into heaven on a chariot of flames, and Ezekiel saw your divinity descend to earth on the same—a chariot of flames.

What is this chariot that runs the course between heaven and earth?

What is this fiery bridge that spans the division wrought by our first parents' sin, a chasm we deepen daily by our failures to love?

The chariot is love.

It is your love for us that brings you down. It is your love for us, overflowing. It is your love in yourself—Father, Son, and Spirit—pouring forth in super-abundance and fecundity, that sent the Son on his divine mission into the world. It is love that stretched his toes toward the earth and his head up to heaven as he hung upon the cross. Love, through suffering, returns us back to you.

A chariot of flame—the Son rode down to earth in love, and in love, he carries us back into your embrace.

So with love, we pray:

Our Father, who art in Heaven
Hallowed be thy name.
Thy kingdom come,
thy will be done,
on earth as it is in heaven.
Give us this day our daily bread,
And forgive us our trespasses,
as we forgive those who trespass against us.
Lead us not into temptation,
But deliver us from evil.
Amen.

Day 20: Immanence

Father, we pray: your will be done on earth as it is in heaven.

At times, Father, your will seems so transcendent—so vast, so gracious, so glorious—that it feels farther away than the heavens, incomprehensible, unknown, distant. Not something that walks alongside us. Not something we can walk alongside.

But your will is not only transcendent, nor is its action only in heaven. For your Son has taught us to pray that it might also be done on earth.

The division we have seen is the fault of our first parents. But if we think of them, we realize you are not always so far away. You walked with them in the garden. You were close. Your will was easily, readily known: Keep and till, be stewards, offer me the worship of your care for my creation. Only one thing—do not eat of that fruit. And yet, eat we did.

O Father, you sent your Son, your Word Incarnate, to walk among us, to remind us of your immanence, of your presence at our side. Your will is not something distant, unknown, too mysterious or hidden for us to grasp. No, your will is written even within our hearts.

What was unclear has been made bright in the Son. The rays of the Sun of Justice have shone—once in a babe at Bethlehem, in splendor on Mount Tabor, with sorrow as darkness covered the earth when he breathed his last, and then with glory again, as death did not last.

Thanks be to you, Father. We know you are not far away. Rather, your will is nearer to us than we are to ourselves.

So, with confidence, we pray:

Our Father, who art in Heaven
Hallowed be thy name.
Thy kingdom come,
thy will be done,
***on earth** as it is in heaven.*
Give us this day our daily bread,
And forgive us our trespasses,
as we forgive those who trespass against us.
Lead us not into temptation,
But deliver us from evil.
Amen.

Day 21: Our Wills

Father, we begin to turn our gaze—not only to you and your action in the heavens and on earth, but to what we ourselves must do. To what we ourselves now desire to do, having been captured by your love.

Father.

Father.

You are Father—which means we are sons and daughters. But what kind of sons? What kind of daughters? What attitude can we have toward such a gracious Father—so grand, so great, so near, so caring—as to give us our firstborn Brother? You do not desire a servant for your Son who has called us friends. You do not wish for a slave, for He has given His life to make us free. No, you wish to have sons and daughters—true children, day by day.

Let us not approach you with the fear of one who must obey, but with the trust of a child, arms upraised and crying: Father. Abba. I love you. I trust you. Supersede all servile fear. Give us the heart of a child, a heart of love, a will that is your own.

While we trust you so dearly, so nearly, let us not resign ourselves to fatalism, as though one man's fall has sealed our fate and the fate of the world.

Let us mount the fiery chariot of love daily, as your sons and daughters, riding around the Sun of Justice, pulling others with that fire into the orbit of His light. Yes, Father, though we must remain here on earth a little while longer, let your will be done in us, through us, as it is in our eldest Brother in heaven.

> *Our Father, who art in Heaven*
> *Hallowed be thy name.*
> *Thy kingdom come,*
> ***thy will be done,***
> ***on earth as it is in heaven.***
> *Give us this day our daily bread,*
> *And forgive us our trespasses,*
> *as we forgive those who trespass against us.*
> *Lead us not into temptation,*
> *But deliver us from evil.*
> *Amen.*

Give us this Day
our Daily Bread

Day 22: Trust

Father, as we turn to you—with our eyes still fixed on you—we begin to plead for ourselves:

Give us this day our daily bread. Help us to believe that you truly desire to give us good gifts. Your Son, who lived among us, taught us that you will never hand us a snake when we ask for a loaf of bread. And so, we ask for bread, Father.

But oh—help us to trust.

We, who have been betrayed and abandoned so many times—Help us to trust you, Father: Your providence, your care, and your attention to our needs.

Not just in the big picture—though certainly that—But even more, in the smallest detail: The tiniest need, the most intimate plea. You are the Father who has counted every hair on our heads.

Father, help us to believe.

Help us to trust fully in your providence, O Father, planned before the ages for our good. Indeed, when we see that all of creation was made for the glory of your only-begotten Son, how could we not believe that You, who provided everything for Him, would also provide everything for us, who are in Him?

Yes, Father—we believe. Help our unbelief.

We trust—help our distrust.

We pray: give us this day our daily bread—and today, that means the grace to trust that you will provide all things. You, who are so good,

> *Our Father, who art in Heaven*
> *Hallowed be thy name.*
> *Thy kingdom come,*
> *thy will be done,*
> *on earth as it is in heaven.*
> ***Give us this day our daily bread,***
> *And forgive us our trespasses,*
> *as we forgive those who trespass against us.*
> *Lead us not into temptation,*
> *But deliver us from evil.*
> *Amen.*

Day 23: Manna in the Desert

Heavenly Father, You know each hair on our heads, each detail of our lives. You desire to provide for us in everything. Indeed, this is one of the things You have been trying to show us from the very beginning. When you brought our forefathers in faith out of Egypt and led them through the desert wilderness for forty years, You fed them daily with manna from above. Like hoarfrost upon the desert floor, you gave them always enough for each day—no more, no less. No matter how much they gathered, You provided exactly the amount they needed.

From the experience of the ancient Israelites, help us to trust that You will provide, each day, exactly what we need. Help us to see, Father, that it is not our taking or collecting that secures our sufficiency, but your providence that supplies everything for us.

When Israel entered the Promised Land and the manna ceased, You still continued to provide—now through the fruit of the earth, from the very land you had promised them and which they now possessed. You gave them what they needed. And even when they rebelled against your kingship, when they begged for themselves an earthly king—through that king, you still provided their daily bread.

Did not the prophets foretell that when the Messiah came, he would provide daily bread for all your beloved people, for all of Israel?

O Father, you have sent the Messiah. You sent him in Jesus Christ.

And He indeed provides our daily bread.

Through Him—our mediator—you give us all things, everything that we need. So help us to trust in His sufficiency for us. Help us to see that just as You once cared for the needs of Your people in the desert, and in the kingdom, and in the land You had promised, so now You provide for us—Your sons and daughters—through the ministry and mystery of your Son, Jesus Christ. Help us to trust You—You who are…

> *Our Father, who art in Heaven*
> *Hallowed be thy name.*
> *Thy kingdom come,*
> *thy will be done,*
> *on earth as it is in heaven.*
> **Give us this day our daily bread,**
> *And forgive us our trespasses,*
> *as we forgive those who trespass against us.*
> *Lead us not into temptation,*
> *But deliver us from evil.*
> *Amen.*

Day 24: Daily Bread

God our Father, for our daily bread, You give us your only begotten Son, Jesus, from the Most Holy Sacrament of the Altar. He left Himself under disguise of bread and wine so that the divine presence might never depart from us: Behold, I am with you even to the end of the age.

Father, we thank you today for this gift—your Son Jesus, present to us in the Eucharist. We ask pardon for all the times we have passed by a tabernacle or received Him on our tongues without discerning His true presence, without discerning the great gift of our sanctification. If we have ever received Him unworthily, we ask now for your pardon and peace.

We ask for the grace and conviction to never approach Him again without soundness of conscience. Together with this, we ask for the grace to trust completely in your mercy, for the same mercy which redeems us on the Cross sanctifies us in the Sacrament.

Father, let us trust in that mercy.

Let us hope in that mercy.

Let us love you in that mercy, as we receive every day our waybread, our food for the journey, in the Eucharist.

Grant us hearts that long for the Sacrament, as we say:

Our Father, who art in Heaven
Hallowed be thy name.
Thy kingdom come,
thy will be done,
on earth as it is in heaven.
*Give us this day **our daily bread,***
And forgive us our trespasses,
as we forgive those who trespass against us.
Lead us not into temptation,
But deliver us from evil.
Amen.

Day 25: Daily Need

Give us this day our daily bread—this day, this moment, we are in need. True, our entire existence depends on your love and hangs in the balance of your willing it. We often proceed without an awareness at a shallow spiritual depth. Yet we are acutely aware of our daily needs: our need for food, for clothing, for shelter.

How often do we fast for but a few hours and begin to call out in need? How often are we outside, bitten by mosquitoes, stung by the wind, or shivering in the cold for only a few minutes—perhaps a walk to the car—and acquire again a sense of our need, a sense of our frail nature?

Father, we need you and your providence to sustain us. Have we not seen that you feed us in the spiritual bread of your Son's Body and Blood in the Eucharist? On the foundation of this experience, we cry also for our bodily food—yes, the nourishment we need for each day—but also for the rest, the recreation, the care, the love which you in your providence arrange for us.

Father, please grant us today our daily needs, the needs of our humanity. You have gifted us with existence; gift us also with everything we need to carry on through today, from the smallest motivations, the smallest of physical satisfactions, to the greatest of our spiritual yearnings and hungers for you.

Our Father, who art in Heaven
Hallowed be thy name.
Thy kingdom come,
thy will be done,
on earth as it is in heaven.
*Give us **this day** our daily bread,*
And forgive us our trespasses,
as we forgive those who trespass against us.
Lead us not into temptation,
But deliver us from evil.
Amen.

Day 26: *Epiousion*

Father, why did your son teach us to pray daily for our *daily* bread?

There is a treasure hidden in this repetition. We daily pray for *epiousion* bread–supersubstantial bread.

What is this super-substance that you desire to give us so much that you taught us to ask for it? It is the Sacrament of our Salvation–the very body and blood, soul and divinity of your firstborn, our eldest brother, Jesus!

These last days we have meditated on your providence for us in both material and spiritual matters; here, in the super-substance of the Eucharist, we find matter and spirit joined together in the great miracle of nourishment, which indeed is remembered daily on the altars of your Church.

Oh Father, feed us with this great gift! Give us more striking hunger, more desperate thirst for this food and drink that carries us to eternal life, that makes us one with you in your Son! Send your Spirit to inflame us with an ever deeper, ever more striking, ever more pressing love that can only be satisfied here below in the brief moments of our communions!

Oh, thank you Father, for sending your Son as our Brother, for feeding us with his flesh and giving us life with his blood! Let us become what we receive; as we receive your Child, may we be ever more truly your children!

Our Father, who art in Heaven
Hallowed be thy name.
Thy kingdom come,
thy will be done,
on earth as it is in heaven.
*Give us this day our **daily** bread,*
And forgive us our trespasses,
as we forgive those who trespass against us.
Lead us not into temptation,
But deliver us from evil.
Amen.

Day 27: Broken for All

Father, we cannot fail to remember that our daily bread, Jesus Christ, was broken for all.

Let us not take for granted the gift of this breaking.

Let us not receive the fruit with no thought for the labor of the sowing and the reaping.

And let us not be satisfied with holding the reward to ourselves alone.

The plowmen dug furrows on his back with their scourges. Let us not let any of the fruit of such a terrible sacrifice go to waste; let us invite all to come and eat at the banquet that was prepared for them!

Yes Father, give us evangelical hearts!

Having received so good a gift from so gracious a giver, let us now join in the work of distributing the good news to all with ears to hear and eyes to see!

Let us join in the planting and the harvest through our prayer, our suffering, and our preaching in word and deed!

And just as we do not keep this most heavenly food to ourselves, may we train ourselves in generosity through sharing also the earthly food you have given in your providence. Let us place all our goods at the foot of the Cross and beg you to distribute them as you will, to give us wisdom to care for all those in need, charity to nourish them in body through mercy and soul through preaching!

Yes, Lord, give us the strength–in that Bread Broken for All, our Brother–to love all those around us!

Our Father, who art in Heaven
Hallowed be thy name.
Thy kingdom come,
thy will be done,
on earth as it is in heaven.
*Give us this day our daily **bread,***
And forgive us our trespasses,
as we forgive those who trespass against us.
Lead us not into temptation,
But deliver us from evil.
Amen.

Forgive us our Trespasses,
as we Forgive

Day 28: Our Need for Forgiveness

Father, forgive us our trespasses, as we forgive those who trespass against us.

A new petition, and yet one that echoes the whole Gospel.

Father, your Son taught us to pray for forgiveness.

But before we can ask, we must see. Illuminate us in the light of your love—and give us the courage to face our sinfulness.

Show us, Father, the hates we've harbored, the despairs we've nursed.

Show us our self-wrought iniquity, the ways we love so little.

Show us our laziness, our disordered desires, our clinging to the world and its comforts.

Show us the evils we choose—even when we know your good.

Grant us, Father, the grace to face the truth: we are sinners.

Shower us with illumination, that we may feel deeply and clearly our need for mercy. Let us not run from our sinfulness but surrender it to the fire of your love. Burn away our imperfections, like dross in the furnace, that we might shine more purely, as gold tested by fire.

Yes, Father, grant us the grace to know our need for your mercy. And grant us, too, the grace to trust in it.

> *Our Father, who art in Heaven*
> *Hallowed be thy name.*
> *Thy kingdom come,*
> *thy will be done,*
> *on earth as it is in heaven.*
> *Give us this day our daily bread,*
> *And **forgive us** our trespasses,*
> *as we forgive those who trespass against us.*
> *Lead us not into temptation,*
> *But deliver us from evil.*
> *Amen.*

Day 29: Our Trespasses

Father, what are our trespasses? They are every moment we fail to live in your love, to live out your love, to love your love.

We've seen already that sin breaks relationships—with your creation, with our neighbors, with you, and even with ourselves. Lord, how do I sin against your creation? Where do I betray it by trying to make it into you—by turning created things into idols? Where do I fail to care for it, and instead exploit it, misuse it through gluttony or laziness? Show me, Lord, my trespasses.

Lord, how do I fail to love my neighbor? Where do I take advantage of them? Where do I nurse hatred or inflict harm? Worse still—where do I simply not care? Where do I pass them by, unseen? Show me those I have overlooked. Reconcile me to those I find so hard to love.

Father, turn me back to you. Help me see your goodness again, so that I may desire to love you more. Send your Spirit—fill me with your love.

And perhaps hardest of all, Lord, show me where I've failed to love myself in you; not the world's love of self, but your pure, healing, restoring love. Make my expectations for myself your expectations. Make my love for myself your love for me. Make all my choices direct me toward your greater glory—knowing that your glory is a human being fully alive.

Our Father, who art in Heaven
Hallowed be thy name.
Thy kingdom come,
thy will be done,
on earth as it is in heaven.
Give us this day our daily bread,
*And forgive us **our trespasses,***
as we forgive those who trespass against us.
Lead us not into temptation,
But deliver us from evil.
Amen.

Day 30: As we Forgive?

Father, why did you place a condition on forgiveness?

Don't you know our weakness? Our inability to move on, to forgive?

Why did you say that you would forgive only as we forgive?

It is because it is only in forgiving that we learn to allow ourselves to be forgiven.

If we do not practice mercy toward others, we won't believe that you will have it for us. If we cannot learn to forgive totally, we will never allow you to forgive us.

Father, open our hearts to forgiveness. Open them to forgiving those who have trespassed against us, so that they may also be open to your forgiveness for our trespasses.

Father, it is so hard—so hard to forgive those who have hurt us or those we love.

So hard to let mercy drive out hate, to let mercy drive out sadness and anger.

Lord, teach us how to be merciful, so that we may be recipients of your mercy.

Teach us how to forgive, so that we may be forgiven.

Our Father, who art in Heaven
Hallowed be thy name.
Thy kingdom come,
thy will be done,
on earth as it is in heaven.
Give us this day our daily bread,
And forgive us our trespasses,
as we forgive those who trespass against us.
Lead us not into temptation,
But deliver us from evil.
Amen.

Day 31: As You Forgive

Father, let your mercy—incarnate in your Son—be the model of our forgiveness. How did you forgive? Teach us to forgive as you forgive. So let us see your forgiveness.

You are so patient. How often did the patriarchs fail to live out your commandments? Even Abraham was impatient in awaiting your promise. How often did Israel wound your heart—through disobedience, through defiance, even asking for a worldly king? How often did they turn to idols? And yet you remained faithful, even as they were unfaithful.

You knew the time would come to send your Son—Jesus, the Messiah. And how did He forgive? He forgave fully.

He ate with tax collectors and prostitutes.

He embraced the lepers.

He raised the dead.

His mercy was an overflowing torrent—seen in his closeness, his identification with our suffering.

Ultimately, he suffered. He was tortured. He died, and was buried—for the forgiveness of our sins. What began as solidarity went so far as suffering and death—so that others could be forgiven. Lord… dare we ask? Give us the grace to forgive to this extreme. Beyond even solidarity, into suffering. Even for our enemies.

Our Father, who art in Heaven
Hallowed be thy name.
Thy kingdom come,
thy will be done,
on earth as it is in heaven.
Give us this day our daily bread,
And forgive us our trespasses,
as we forgive those who trespass against us.
Lead us not into temptation,
But deliver us from evil.
Amen.

Day 32: Counting the Cost

Father, we sometimes hear a different word in this petition—not trespasses, but debts.

Debts are what is owed.

Why is this image so powerful? Because you know exactly how much is owed. You know the weight of every sin. You know the full cost of our trespasses. Jesus knew the size of the debt he came to repay—he knew it completely.

So also, Father, grant us the courage to examine exactly how much others' trespasses have injured us. Let us see the cost of their transgression—not to demand it, but to know it, so that we may forgive it in full.

Grant us the strength to walk with you into the depths of our pain and suffering at the hands of others, so that we may know how much is being forgiven—and leave nothing unpaid, nothing carried, nothing buried.

Let it be paid not by vengeance but by mercy.

Knowing exactly how deeply we've been wounded, allow us to turn entirely to your healing mercy. Let us follow your example—not of exacting payment, but of forgiving a debt.

Our Father, who art in Heaven
Hallowed be thy name.
Thy kingdom come,
thy will be done,
on earth as it is in heaven.
Give us this day our daily bread,
And forgive us our trespasses,
*as **we forgive those who trespass against us.***
Lead us not into temptation,
But deliver us from evil.
Amen.

Day 33: Divine Mercy

Father, your mercy is great. And as we have prayed with you, we have begun to see just how great it truly is.

On Good Friday, we saw how far you were willing to go—allowing your Son to suffer and give his life for the forgiveness of our sins.

Grant us full trust and hope in that mercy, Lord. But keep us from the snare of presumption—the lie that you will forgive us even when we do not want you to.

Let us seek your forgiveness freely, not out of fear, but with faith.

Let us not be scrupulous or unbelieving.

Let us never think that our sin is too great to be swallowed in the ocean of your mercy.

Father, let us stand beneath the blood and water that flowed from the side of your Son, lifted high on the cross. Yes, Lord—wash us in the blood and water from His side. The blood and water of divine love. The blood and water of mercy.

Let us turn to you in confession.

Let us turn to you for the forgiveness of our sins.

Let us trust the instruments you have given us for our salvation—the sacraments.

Let us trust the daily actions of our life of faith; not so much in the actions themselves as in the grace that works through them.

Father, let us trust totally.

Let us entrust ourselves totally to the greatness of your mercy.

Our Father, who art in Heaven
Hallowed be thy name.
Thy kingdom come,
thy will be done,
on earth as it is in heaven.
Give us this day our daily bread,
And forgive us our trespasses,
as we forgive those who trespass against us.
Lead us not into temptation,
But deliver us from evil.
Amen.

Day 34: The Heart

Father, the Sacred Heart of your Son is an image of your mercy. Pierced, bleeding, wounded, and defiled, it reminds us completely of his love, his identification with us in our humanity, and of his forgiveness of our sins through his divinity.

Father, we beg you: replace our hearts with his.

Give us his heart with which to love.

Give us his heart with which to forgive, so that we, too, may be forgiven.

Give us Mary's pure heart, so that we may not sin.

Give us Joseph's chaste heart, so that we might love as he loved.

Father, draw us into your heart.

Let us take up our home in your love.

Let us live our lives in the inner room of your heart.

Let us be icons, merciful icons, of the Sacred Heart to the world.

Just as that image reminds us of Christ's mercy—and therefore, yours—let us become images of forgiveness and reconciliation that remind the world of You.

Our Father, who art in Heaven
Hallowed be thy name.
Thy kingdom come,
thy will be done,
on earth as it is in heaven.
Give us this day our daily bread,
And forgive us our trespasses,
as we forgive those who trespass against us.
Lead us not into temptation,
But deliver us from evil.
Amen.

88

Lead us not into Temptation

Day 35: The Danger of Backsliding

Oh, good Father—as we now turn to reflect on the petition, "Lead us not into temptation," first remind us: you are a good Father who welcomes us back, even as prodigal children.

But even as we trust in your mercy, let us not be presumptuous.

Father, help us to see that we must strive and struggle to walk toward you each day. For all your sons and daughters—our Christian brothers and sisters, the saints and spiritual masters—have taught us that we either walk toward you or away from you in every moment. To stand still is not a Christian option.

So Father, having begged your forgiveness, having entrusted ourselves totally to your mercy, let us now pray fervently that even while we will always need your mercy, we may not backslide—may not return to our former sins, or fall into even worse than before.

Yes, Father, we daily need a deeper conversion— whether that means conversion from mortal sin to grace, or the more difficult conversion: from the acceptable to the better, or the better to the best.

Let us walk more firmly in the footsteps of your Son.

Let us not turn back when we face trials and temptations—or perhaps the most dangerous snare of all: simple tiredness, the loss of fire, the slow, quiet fading of our desire to keep fighting, to love you more and more. Yes, Father—inflame us anew each day with a deeper desire for charity, with a greater ability to walk in the footsteps of your Son, our Lord, Jesus Christ.

Our Father, who art in Heaven
Hallowed be thy name.
Thy kingdom come,
thy will be done,
on earth as it is in heaven.
Give us this day our daily bread,
And forgive us our trespasses,
as we forgive those who trespass against us.
Lead us not into temptation,
But deliver us from evil.
Amen.

Day 36: You Tempt Us?

Holy Father, please send your Spirit to grant us a spirit of discernment as we face the trials and temptations of life. Grant us the grace to distinguish—between trials, which you allow for our strengthening, and temptations, which never come from you.

Trials are opportunities to grow—to train our spiritual muscles: our faith, our trust, our hope, and our love.

Temptations, though, come from the world, the flesh, and the devil. They seek to lead us away from the one Way—your Son, Jesus Christ.

Yes, Father, help us to discern not only between trials and temptations, but also between temptation and consent. Let us not be scrupulous but let us also never presume. Let us be trusting sons and daughters, who walk in the light—the one light of your grace.

Father, we know you are a good Father, who gives only good gifts. You do not tempt us. At times, you may allow us to be tested—through the consequences of our own choices, through the promptings and vile schemes of the enemy, or through the tangled appetites of the world's ways. But you do not tempt us. Help us believe that. Help us recognize temptations for what they are—

snares set in our path to lead us away from you. Strengthen our wills, that we may reject temptations at every turn. Let us see them quickly. Let us flee them promptly—by calling upon your name.

Our Father, who art in Heaven
Hallowed be thy name.
Thy kingdom come,
thy will be done,
on earth as it is in heaven.
Give us this day our daily bread,
And forgive us our trespasses,
as we forgive those who trespass against us.
*Lead us not into **temptation**,*
But deliver us from evil.
Amen.

Day 37: Fasting

Good Father, you sent your Son to show us the way to you. Part of that showing was serving as an example. Even as we pray that we may not enter into temptation, we know that temptations will come. We know this because they came even for your Son. Indeed, before his public ministry began, he went into the desert where he did battle for forty days and forty nights with the ancient foe, our enemy, Satan. And what were the weapons he used to fight? The proven practices: prayer and fasting. Today, Father, let us focus on fasting.

So many things we simply accept—perhaps not sinful in themselves, but small comforts that dull our hunger for you:

That extra little pleasure.

That extra hour of sleep.

That soda.

That dessert.

That cooling drink.

That savory delight on the tongue.

That image we crave.

That extra minute scrolling.

That one more page.

That one more screen.

None of these are you.

And when they are not handled with care, they become gateways—not to rest, but to despair.

Help us to fast, Lord.

Not because these things are evil, but because they are not our end. Because, as Augustine warns, we must not let the good things found along the way distract us from our true homeland. Help us to fast, that we might train ourselves to stand strong in the face of temptation—knowing that you will never allow us to be tested beyond what we can bear.

Father, show us today what we need to fast from. Help us to be obedient to the Church's little practices of penance, like Friday abstinence. Help us to discern what things become doorways, occasions of sin, and help us to put them aside, to fast from them, to flee from them—even if only for a time—so that we might not be distracted from our true destination: our home with you.

Our Father, who art in Heaven
Hallowed be thy name.
Thy kingdom come,
thy will be done,
on earth as it is in heaven.
Give us this day our daily bread,
And forgive us our trespasses,
as we forgive those who trespass against us.
Lead us not into temptation,
But deliver us from evil.
Amen.

Day 38: Prayer

Heavenly Father, grant us the grace today to remember the necessity of prayer. Prayer is not optional. It is the very breath of our spiritual life. And without it, we will have no strength to stand against temptation.

If prayer is where we enter into communion with you—with your Son, and with the Spirit—if it is where we draw our very breath, then to neglect it is to walk into battle gasping for air. How can one drowning in worldly anxieties, in the minutiae and monotony of everyday life—how can that one stand firm if they never turn aside to breathe in your presence?

How can one who has no air in their lungs have any strength to fight when temptation comes?

How can one who never practices handing over their cares to you each day suddenly trust you when trial strikes?

They cannot.

Very simply, they cannot.

So, Lord, grant us the grace to pray every single day. As we say, "Lead us not into temptation," we recognize that this must be more than words—it must be backed by a life of prayer. So, Lord, teach us not only how to pray, but that we must pray. Let today be a day—perhaps for the first time, or perhaps a return—when we set aside our hour with you, our portion, our first fruits. Let us be bold. Let us entrust ourselves totally to your care.

Because if we do not pray—if we do not give you the best part of our day—then our words, "Lead us not into temptation," will be just that: words. A wish. A gesture. Empty.

So, Lord, as we say, "Lead us not into temptation," we add this prayer beside it: Grant us the grace to make time to pray.

Our Father, who art in Heaven
Hallowed be thy name.
Thy kingdom come,
thy will be done,
on earth as it is in heaven.
Give us this day our daily bread,
And forgive us our trespasses,
as we forgive those who trespass against us.
Lead us not into temptation,
But deliver us from evil.
Amen.

Day 39: Almsgiving

Father, having considered prayer and fasting as ways we can cooperate with you—so as not to be led into temptation—we now turn our attention to almsgiving. Just as fasting helps us turn away from comforts for a time, just as prayer draws us daily into communion with you, so too almsgiving becomes a form of Christian training—a preparation for battle. Giving of ourselves, giving of our goods to those more in need—this, too, strengthens us for the trials to come.

And so, Father, we ask you: teach us how to give.

Teach us to offer the first portion to your Son present in the poor, the needy, the downtrodden, the oppressed. You began teaching this long ago, to Abraham, and to our ancestors in the faith. If Abraham could tithe a tenth of his goods to Melchizedek, your servant, then how much more should we give—we who face not just temporal struggle, but the possibility of eternal loss, if we do not seek your help in resisting temptation?

Give us eyes, Father, to see your face in the poor. Grant us the freedom to give, so that nothing may become a snare to us. Let there be no attachment, no grasping, but only overflowing, abundant charity—

fostered by a life rooted in you.

And in loving you and our neighbor, may we be strengthened to stand against all temptations.

Our Father, who art in Heaven
Hallowed be thy name.
Thy kingdom come,
thy will be done,
on earth as it is in heaven.
Give us this day our daily bread,
And forgive us our trespasses,
as we forgive those who trespass against us.
Lead us not into temptation,
But deliver us from evil.
Amen.

100

Deliver us from Evil

Day 40: Perseverance

Father, as we now transition to the closely related petition—that you would deliver us from evil—we pause to reflect on the hinge that connects these two prayers.

Between "Lead us not into temptation" and "Deliver us from evil," stands the grace of perseverance.

In both petitions, we speak as those who have already received your mercy—having prayed for forgiveness, having been justified by grace. But now, we ask not just for mercy once, but for the strength to endure. We pray not to backslide, not to fall away from the path you have set before us. We beg you, Father, deliver us from the assaults of the evil one.

We do not pray so that our lives might be easy, peaceful, or free of difficulty.

We pray so that we may persevere, which is to endure, to stay faithful, to come into your kingdom in its fullness at the final resurrection.

We pray that no stumbling block, no stone, may trip us up as we follow you.

That no evil may dissuade us from your way.

That no weariness or sorrow may turn us aside.

We pray, Father, that we may continue, that we may

persevere. And we know—because Holy Mother Church teaches us—that this is a grace. A gift. It is not to be presumed, not to be taken for granted.

Let us never assume that having once turned to you is enough.

Let us not think that saying "Our Father" once with our lips means we need not live it daily with our lives.

No—grant us the grace of final perseverance so that we may remain faithful, united to your Son, conformed to his image until the end.

We ask this grace not only for ourselves, but for all those we love.

Let nothing drive our hand from the plow.

Let nothing turn our gaze over our shoulder.

Let us keep walking, step by step, after your Son.

Our Father, who art in Heaven
Hallowed be thy name.
Thy kingdom come,
thy will be done,
on earth as it is in heaven.
Give us this day our daily bread,
And forgive us our trespasses,
as we forgive those who trespass against us.
Lead us not into temptation,
But deliver us from evil.
Amen.

Day 41: The Strange Reality of Evil

Good Father, we must face up to an uncomfortable fact of our experience: as we go through life, we encounter evil. For something that is the absence of good, evil has a strange potency.

Natural evils come and go—illness, disaster, decay. These are hard enough to endure, hard enough to accept and surrender to you.

But that stranger, more haranguing potency is the evil found in the will: in our own wills, in the wills of our neighbors, in the wills of demons. This evil, though parasitic—though it has no being of its own—takes on a kind of painful presence.

It wounds.

It haunts.

It is hard to endure.

And harder still to surrender to you.

But, Lord, we must remember: you are the Deliverer from evil. The ancient Israelites too often turned to themselves, demanding kings, or looking to foreign powers like Egypt to save them from their enemies. Let us not follow that bad example. Let us not turn inward to ourselves alone, or outward to worldly solutions alone, as though they could truly confront evil.

No, Father, let us trust in you.

Let us trust in your power to save. Even as we do what little we can, as we work for justice, as we resist evil with our choices, let our trust be totally in you. Let us surrender to your saving power in Jesus Christ, your Son—he who has already conquered sin and death, he who has already defeated the evil one.

Our Father, who art in Heaven
Hallowed be thy name.
Thy kingdom come,
thy will be done,
on earth as it is in heaven.
Give us this day our daily bread,
And forgive us our trespasses,
as we forgive those who trespass against us.
Lead us not into temptation,
But deliver us from evil.
Amen.

Day 42: The Enemy

Father, grant us grace and peace as we rest in your protecting arms—trusting in your strength, your love, and your constancy.

We acknowledge a hard truth: we have an enemy. An ancient foe. The devil. Satan, who desires nothing but our destruction. This is not a pleasant reality. But it is one we must face—so that we may realize how much we need your help.

Our enemy is more clever than we are. He knows how to manipulate us. He knows our weaknesses. And he hates us. We need you.

So, Lord—deliver us.

Truly, Lord, we beg for your help.

You alone are the one who conquers him.

You alone can grant us victory.

You alone defend us in the daily battle for our salvation.

Without giving the enemy too much focus, without obsessing over him, let us also not feign false security—as if we were stronger or smarter than he. Instead, graft us securely to the true vine—Jesus Christ, your Son, our Brother. Let us entrust our lives, our battles, our very selves to you, in Him.

Father, we pray: deliver us from the evil one.

Our Father, who art in Heaven
Hallowed be thy name.
Thy kingdom come,
thy will be done,
on earth as it is in heaven.
Give us this day our daily bread,
And forgive us our trespasses,
as we forgive those who trespass against us.
Lead us not into temptation,
But deliver us from evil.
Amen.

Day 43: No Comparison

Father, in these past days, we've been reflecting on the reality of evil—on the fact that we do have an enemy, on the need to pray for perseverance. But now, Father, teach us anew: there is no comparison between you and evil. You are greater.

Help us to reject any inclination to believe that you and evil stand on equal footing—that you and the evil one are rival powers, somehow locked in a contest.

No.

There is no contest.

No rivalry.

No tension between two equal forces.

This is not a battle where we wait to see who wins.

No—this is a victory already won.

The Paschal Mystery has already declared the outcome. The victory belongs to Christ. The evil one is not a challenger—but a defeated enemy, a sore loser, throwing a tantrum until time is complete.

Father, you are good.

You are great.

You can deliver us from the evil one—and we trust that you will.

We know that you are stronger.

We know that good is victorious.

Where we struggle to believe this, where our faith is thin or our hope flickers—grant us deeper faith.

Grant us firmer hope.

And above all, grant us perfect charity—the kind of love that casts out all fear.

Even as we acknowledge the reality of the evil one, the presence of evil in the world, the suffering it can cause, let us not fear. For you are

Our Father, who art in Heaven
Hallowed be thy name.
Thy kingdom come,
thy will be done,
on earth as it is in heaven.
Give us this day our daily bread,
And forgive us our trespasses,
as we forgive those who trespass against us.
Lead us not into temptation,
*But **deliver us** from evil.*
Amen.

Day 44: Paschal Mystery, Final Victory

Father, you sent your only begotten Son into the world so that all creation might be gathered and consecrated in him, so that he might be the firstborn among many brothers, so that we might become your family. But first of all, you sent him for his own glory, that He Himself might be glorified. His mother, Mary, stands second to him. His foster father, Joseph, in the third place.

And yet, even though you sent your Son first for his own glory, you also sent him because humanity stood in need of redemption. Our first parents had fallen. And so, your Son came to redeem. He freely gave himself, submitting to your will in the Garden of Gethsemane, so that we might be redeemed—through his Passion, his death on the Cross, his descent into hell, his Resurrection, his Ascension, and the sending of the Holy Spirit.

Through the Paschal Mystery, we have been redeemed.

And what's more—the evil one has been conquered and cast down. He has no power left over those who live in Christ.

And even more wonderfully still—we have been lifted to a greater dignity than that which we had before the Fall. The state of redemption is greater than the state of original innocence.

Father, we thank you. Because in Christ, you have already delivered us from evil. We pray now that the grace of that deliverance may take root in our hearts: may flower into holiness, may become beautiful in our lives, in our Redeemer, Jesus Christ, whose members we now are, as his Mystical Body. Yes, Father—thank you for the gift of the Paschal Mystery, which is our everlasting victory.

Our Father, who art in Heaven
Hallowed be thy name.
Thy kingdom come,
thy will be done,
on earth as it is in heaven.
Give us this day our daily bread,
And forgive us our trespasses,
as we forgive those who trespass against us.
Lead us not into temptation,
But deliver us from evil.
Amen.

Doxology

Day 45: Thine is the Kingdom

Father, your daughter, the Church, includes a final phrase when she prays the Lord's Prayer in the Mass: "For the kingdom, the power, and the glory are yours, now and forever." Father, help us to remember the kingdom—the kingdom we prayed for so many days ago.

We live in a new reality now, a life that bridges heaven and earth through the mystery of sacramentality. We no longer belong to this world, even as we live in it. The powers and principalities of the earth do not have the final claim on our lives.

No, our King is Christ.

Our Messiah is Jesus.

And he alone has the ultimate claim on us. But he does not call us slaves. He does not call us mere servants. He calls us friends as we do what you, Father, command.

So, we beg again: give us the grace to understand, to live, and to love as you command. Make us, every day, more and more your sons and daughters in the one Son, Jesus Christ. Make us, each in our own vocation and station, living members of the Mystical Body of your Son, participants in his reign. Not merely subjects but heirs.

Heirs of the grace and glory which you, Father, have

willed for us from all eternity.

Heirs alongside the saints, whose identity for all time is to be the siblings of your Son, your children, forever.

Our Father, who art in Heaven
Hallowed be thy name.
Thy kingdom come,
thy will be done,
on earth as it is in heaven.
Give us this day our daily bread,
And forgive us our trespasses,
as we forgive those who trespass against us.
Lead us not into temptation,
But deliver us from evil..

For the kingdom,
And the power,
And the glory are yours,
Now and forever.

Amen.

Day 46: The Power

Yours, Father, is the power.

Throughout these days, we have prayed with the prayer your Son gave us. Again and again, we have asked for the grace to know, understand, and trust your power. Most recently, we asked for the grace to believe—truly believe—that your power is far greater, incomparably greater, than that of the evil one or of any evil whatsoever.

It is your power that keeps us from falling into temptation.

It is your power, through mercy, that forgives our sins.

It is your power that provides for all our needs—of both body and soul.

It is your power that forms our wills, that inspires our intellects, that becomes our courage in weakness.

It is your power that builds the heavenly kingdom—a kingdom that breaks into our earthly reality through the redeeming work of your Son.

It is your power that reveals You to us throughout all of salvation history.

In fact, Father, you are your power. You are omnipotence. And your power is so great, so glorious, so far beyond what we can even conceive.

Lord, we praise you for your power. We thank you for all the good you have worked through it—in us and for us. You are all-powerful. We do not have a weak Father. We have you, the one who does all things in us so that we might truly be your children. Therefore, with praise and gratitude we say:

> *Our Father, who art in Heaven*
> *Hallowed be thy name.*
> *Thy kingdom come,*
> *thy will be done,*
> *on earth as it is in heaven.*
> *Give us this day our daily bread,*
> *And forgive us our trespasses,*
> *as we forgive those who trespass against us.*
> *Lead us not into temptation,*
> *But deliver us from evil..*

> *For the kingdom,*
> ***And the power,***
> *And the glory are yours,*
> *Now and forever.*

> *Amen.*

Day 47: The Glory

Heavenly Father, yours is the glory. Every time we come together—in the worship of the liturgy, the sacrifice of the Mass, the celebration of the sacraments, the Liturgy of the Hours—we give glory to you, as is truly right and just. The glory is yours. It belongs to you. And in every act of worship and praise, we are not giving you something you lack—we are simply acknowledging what is already true: Yours is the glory.

May our lives become icons of your glory.

May our lives become icons of Christ Jesus, who is your glory made flesh. All things were created for his glory. All things were made through him, redeemed through him, and destined to return to you through him. For His glory is your glory, Father—for You and the Son are one. May we, too, become one in that one glory.

Lord God, our Father, grant your Church unity.

Grant her peace.

May she shine as a beacon of your light, so that all nations might come to know your glory, to trust in your glory, to love you in your glory, and—by grace—become your glory, as they live in imitation of your Son, by the power of your Spirit, and by the gift of your glory.

Our Father, who art in Heaven
Hallowed be thy name.
Thy kingdom come,
thy will be done,
on earth as it is in heaven.
Give us this day our daily bread,
And forgive us our trespasses,
as we forgive those who trespass against us.
Lead us not into temptation,
But deliver us from evil..

For the kingdom,
And the power,
And the glory are yours,
Now and forever.

Amen.

Day 48: Now and Forever

Father, yours is the kingdom, the power, and the glory—now and forever. Now—in this moment, as we pray on this very day:

Yours is the kingdom.

Yours is the power.

Yours is the glory.

No matter what we feel or suffer, no matter how holy we are or are not, we give you the glory *now*.

Help us, Father, to live the grace of this present moment, to praise you in the now, to adore your perfect goodness, your perfect authority, your perfect power, your perfect glory beyond all telling.

Lord God, our Father, give us the grace of this moment to bask in your truth. Give us the grace to love you—to love you in this now.

And at the same time, grant us the hope and faith to believe that the glory of this now, the kingdom of this now, the power of this now, extends forever. From ages to ages, world without end.

Give us, Father, a firm, filial hope—that the goodness of this moment in you is not fleeting, not passing, not like the fragile glories of this world. This goodness is forever.

Let us believe in this up to our final breath.

Let us hope for this up to our ultimate hour.

Let us long for everlasting life in your love, where we may embrace you for all eternity, through the gracious gift of your Son, our Lord Jesus Christ, in whom all things are ours, in whom we are heirs of your kingdom, your power, and your glory, now and forever. Amen.

Our Father, who art in Heaven
Hallowed be thy name.
Thy kingdom come,
thy will be done,
on earth as it is in heaven.
Give us this day our daily bread,
And forgive us our trespasses,
as we forgive those who trespass against us.
Lead us not into temptation,
But deliver us from evil..

For the kingdom,
And the power,
And the glory are yours,
Now and forever.

Amen.

Amen

Day 49: Amen!

Father, as preacher and pray-er, at the close of these days, you have given us the grace and the space to reflect, to meditate, to pray through the prayer your Son taught us. And now we end simply, by saying: Amen.

Amen.

Amen!

So be it.

You are in heaven, Lord.

Amen.

You are our Father. Not mine alone—but the Father of every Christian. Amen.

Your name is holy, Lord. Let me recognize it. Let all the world recognize it. Amen!

Your kingdom come, Lord, so that your rule may be on earth as it is in heaven. Amen, I say, to that.

You truly do give us our daily bread—you nourish us with everything we need, physically and spiritually. Amen.

The Eucharist is your gift—your everlasting presence with us in this age. Amen!

You forgive us our trespasses, and you give us the grace so that we can forgive others. Amen.

You lead us not into temptation—in fact, you help us in our hour of need. So be it. Amen. I believe.

Lord, may you deliver us from evil. Amen.

For yours is the kingdom—so be it.

The power—so be it.

The glory—so be it.

Forever and ever. Amen, Amen, Amen.

May I say more truly every day: I love you, Father, and I live in your love as your beloved son or daughter.

Amen.

Our Father, who art in Heaven
Hallowed be thy name.
Thy kingdom come,
thy will be done,
on earth as it is in heaven.
Give us this day our daily bread,
And forgive us our trespasses,
as we forgive those who trespass against us.
Lead us not into temptation,
But deliver us from evil..

For the kingdom,
And the power,
And the glory are yours,
Now and forever.

Amen.

Oblation to the Father

Day 50: Prayer of Oblation to the Father

Come, Holy Spirit.

Jesus, teach me how to pray.

Father, today I renew the promises of my baptism.

I entrust myself totally to you.

Having already been claimed by you as your son/daughter, guided by the Holy Spirit, and confident in the salvation wrought by your Son—my Brother—I claim you today.

I accept you, submit to you, and love you as my Father.

I set my eyes on the heavenly homeland and submit to you all that I am. I submit my good works—past, present, and future—for the one goal, to be with you forever in your kingdom.

I submit to you my intellect, my memory, my understanding, and my imagination, so that you can reveal your kingdom to me and show me how you desire me to participate in it here below.

I submit to you my will, my passions, my desires, my hopes, and my fears, so that your will may be done in me.

I entrust to you all my needs—whether of body or soul—knowing that you are a good Father who gives every good gift needed to persevere in love and to live a life in the Spirit for the glory of your Son.

Father, I beg you: prevent me from falling into temptation.

Believing that I have been forgiven for all my past sins through sacramental confession and the ministry of the Church, I firmly resolve to sin no more, to strive always for the good, and to avoid every near occasion of sin.

I know that trials and temptations will come. Therefore, I submit myself entirely to your power and your strength—to be my grace in the hour of need.

As your Son once prayed, I too pray: that the hour might pass from me.

But like him, I also pray: Not my will, but yours be done.

Finally, Lord, I profess a deep, sincere, and complete trust that You are my Deliverer from every evil.

I profess that You have already conquered the evil one, and I reject him—all his works, all his pomp, and all his empty show—in favor of your love.

Father, I worship you.

I acknowledge that yours alone is the power, the glory, the kingdom, forever and ever.

Father, I am your little child, now and forever.

Amen.

Afterword

50 days later we have completed our little mystagogy. Return, if you will, to the prayer of St. Francis with which we concluded our *Introduction* and see whether the saint's words are now your own. Having confirmed our trust and love for the Father in Jesus Christ, the One Son, let us continue now on our Christian journey. If this book has helped you in some small measure to develop a habit of mental prayer, then keep on the way! Continue to pray daily to the Father in Spirit and Truth. When you have no material for prayer or dryness steals your desire, return to the *Our Father*. From this one prayer we have drawn so many moments of prayer, without even beginning to exhaust its richness. You have tasted the font of prayer. Now, drink deeply, and be assured that these streams of living water will never run dry. May St. Francis' blessing for Brother Leo be your own:

May the Lord bless you and keep you.
May He show His face to you and be merciful to you.
May He turn His countenance to you
and give you peace.